PICTURES to PARAGRAPHS

WRITING DRAMA

Heather E. Schwartz

Lerner Publications ◆ Minneapolis

Lerner Publications Company
An imprint of Lerner Publishing Group, Inc.
241 First Avenue North
Minneapolis, MN 55401 USA

For reading levels and more information, look up this title at www.lernerbooks.com.

Main body text set in Aptifer Sans LT Pro.
Typeface provided by Linotype AG.

Editor: Nicole Berglund **Designer:** Emily Harris
Lerner team: Martha Kranes

Library of Congress Cataloging-in-Publication Data

Names: Schwartz, Heather E. author
Title: Writing drama / Heather E. Schwartz.
Description: Minneapolis : Lerner Publications, 2026. | Series: Pictures to paragraphs | Includes bibliographical references and index. | Audience: Ages 8–12 | Audience: Grades 4–6 | Summary: "Drama stories are told through scenes and dialogue. Readers discover the different elements of drama and refine their dramatic writing skills with photo prompts"— Provided by publisher.
Identifiers: LCCN 2025016363 (print) | LCCN 2025016364 (ebook) | ISBN 9798765688816 library binding | ISBN 9798348028800 paperback | ISBN 9798765695982 epub
Subjects: LCSH: Playwriting—Juvenile literature
Classification: LCC PN1661 .S387 2026 (print) | LCC PN1661 (ebook) | DDC 808.2—dc23/eng/20250417

LC record available at https://lccn.loc.gov/2025016363
LC ebook record available at https://lccn.loc.gov/2025016364

Manufactured in the United States of America
1-1012676-54711-7/10/2025

TABLE OF CONTENTS

Drama Brings Writing to Life 4

CHAPTER 1
OPENING SCENES 6

CHAPTER 2
RISING ACTION 16

CHAPTER 3
DRAMATIC CONCLUSION 24

Glossary 30
Learn More 31
Index 32

DRAMA BRINGS WRITING TO LIFE

Do you have a favorite TV show? Do you love watching movies, plays, and musicals? These forms of entertainment have a few things in common. They're all considered drama, which tells stories through dialogue and action. The stories are written as a script. Instead of reading them, audiences are meant to watch as they are performed.

The process for writing drama isn't that different from other types of writing. It helps to plan and outline your plot before you start. You can develop your ideas in a draft and share the draft with others to get feedback. After you evaluate your draft, you can revise it to make it better. At the end of the writing process, you can edit your work to make it as perfect as possible.

Some writers publish their work when they're finished. When you're writing drama, you have a unique opportunity. You could ask some classmates and friends to perform it for an audience!

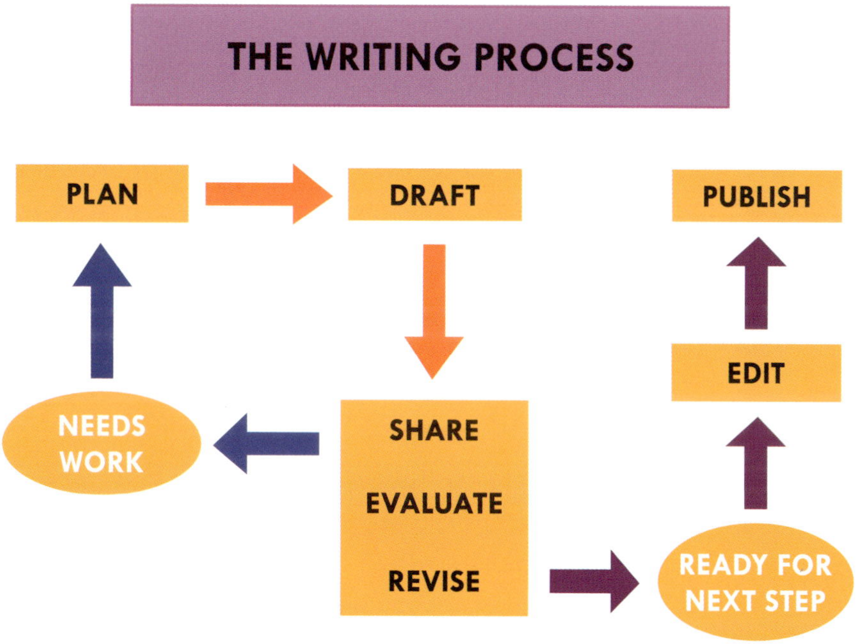

CHAPTER 1

OPENING SCENES

Many dramas have three acts—the introduction, the rising action, and the climax and resolution. The process of writing drama is a little like building a house. You start with a framework—that's the plan or outline for your story. Once you have a plan, you can consider how you will develop the story. You can get creative in how you tell it, similar to how people decorate their house after it is built. Some drama writers plan by listing the scenes they want to include to tell their story. They think about the action that will carry the story forward from beginning to end.

When you're figuring out your story and making your plan, it helps to ask yourself some questions. Who is this story about? What do the characters want? Will the characters get what they want or not?

Your story starts with the opening scenes. Here, the audience meets the characters. Whether those characters are likable or not, people need to care about who they are and what they want. This will keep people interested in your drama. They'll wonder what's going to happen next.

WRITING PROMPT: WHO AND WHAT

Notice the details in this image. What is the person wearing? What is she doing? Use these clues to write a short scene about who this person is and what she wants.

Location and time frame are important in opening scenes too. Where are your characters? When is the action taking place? As the writer, you need to plan the answers to these questions. Your drama could occur in a specific historic period, time of day, or place. Consider what kinds of sets and props would show these details.

WRITING PROMPT: WHERE AND WHEN

Two hikers have been lost in the mountains all day. They are hungry and don't have much gear. Write a short drama describing what might happen when the hikers arrive at this deserted picnic. Make sure to include action that matches this particular environment. Consider the location and time of day as you write.

Dialogue moves a drama along just as much as action does. It can also tell the audience a lot about each character's personality. You can get creative with dialogue by having characters use language in different ways. For example, an outgoing character might be very talkative. You can write basic dialogue to give actors more freedom too. Many dramas allow actors to interpret and experiment. You can also write stage directions to tell actors how to move or react.

Figurative language is fun to use when writing creative dialogue. Maybe one character speaks in metaphors, describing people and places as other things. Perhaps another character uses similes in their speech, comparing people and places to other things using the words *like* or *as*. The character might say a smart person is "as wise as an owl."

If your drama includes someone who speaks a language other than English, they might use some terms many English speakers don't know. You may want to include some lines of dialogue back and forth to explain what the words mean. Or you might decide to leave the other characters—and the audience—confused. That could add mystery or comedy to your drama.

WRITING PROMPT: DIALOGUE FOR DIFFERENT CHARACTERS

Write several lines of dialogue between two characters describing their lunch at school. Have one character use speech filled with metaphors about food. Have the other use speech filled with similes about food.

The mood of your drama should be clear starting in your opening scenes. A drama doesn't have to be serious—it might be funny. Or it could be spooky and suspenseful. Your drama can have any mood you choose. You can show it to the audience through dialogue, action, time, place, and other details.

WRITING PROMPT: SETTING THE MOOD

How does this photo make you feel? Write a short piece that describes how the image puts you in a certain mood. Talk about specific parts of the photo—including the items and colors—and the overall mood they create.

CHAPTER 2
RISING ACTION

Every drama has conflict. On one side, one or more characters want something. On the other side, one or more characters are standing in their way. You can show who the characters are through their dialogue, a monologue or speech, a song, and their actions. Consider each character's perspective and how it impacts what they say and do. What do they want? Why do they want it?

WRITING PROMPT: DIFFERENT PERSPECTIVES

These two images show the same city. Write two short paragraphs describing what you see in each image. Include details such as characters, mood, and location. When you're done, consider how the perspective of each image impacted how you wrote about them.

Once you have your conflict, you can consider how you want to build rising action. Rising action includes the challenges and obstacles that get in your characters' way. Adding more and more of these is called raising the stakes. How will the conflict be resolved?

If it seems as if the conflict is impossible to resolve, that's great! The audience will watch eagerly to see what happens next. As long as the writer knows where the story is headed, it's going in the right direction.

WRITING PROMPT: RAISING THE STAKES

Imagine this character is about to discover something behind the locked door that will make their life more difficult. Write a short scene about what happens next.

In drama, every action and line of dialogue counts. If it doesn't move the story forward, it doesn't belong and should be cut. One way to evaluate your own work is to read it out loud. This can help you hear if there's unnecessary action or dialogue in your draft. You can also use this method to check whether the actions seem as if your characters would do them. You can decide whether the dialogue sounds the way your characters would speak. Evaluating your work will help you decide how you want to revise.

WRITING PROMPT: MAKING CUTS

Imagine a character is late to work and their boss is angry. Write a list of ten excuses for why the character is late. Use this photo to inspire ideas, but feel free to come up with some silly excuses too—such as, "I had to take my pet turtle for a walk, and I just couldn't get her moving." When you're done, choose your top five favorite excuses and cross out the rest to practice making cuts.

Sharing your draft with others can help you evaluate it too. When you share a drama, you have a chance to hear it out loud in a different way. You can cast friends and classmates to read aloud as specific characters.

Listen carefully. Does the dialogue sound like real conversation? Are any of the lines too complicated for your actors? Considering questions such as these can help you figure out how to revise. Other people will have different perspectives on your work. They may offer varied opinions about your draft. Take the advice you believe will make the draft better and use it as you revise.

WRITING PROMPT: WRITER'S CHOICE

This hiker is looking at a map while exploring in the mountains. Does she believe she's headed in the right direction? Or is she worried that she's lost? Choose one of these perspectives to write a short drama about her and what she will do next.

CHAPTER 3
DRAMATIC CONCLUSION

At the height of the rising action, it may seem as if the conflict will never be resolved. This is the climax, where things finally go one way or the other. After that comes the falling action, where loose ends are tied up. It's the writer's job to fit all the pieces together, like a puzzle. Each scene of a drama leads to a logical conclusion.

The end of the writing process is logical too. After evaluating and revising, it makes sense to edit. This is when writers often catch mistakes. These might be spelling and grammatical errors. Maybe a character's name changes halfway through the story. Perhaps a timeline is mixed up. You might discover many mistakes when you're editing, but that's okay. There's still time to fix the problems.

When you edit your writing, you can catch and fix mistakes.

Ending a drama can be challenging—especially after you've raised the stakes, reached a climax, and need to decide how it can all work out. Sometimes, writers wrap things up by saying it was all a dream. But that can feel like a cheat to audiences who care about the characters and the conflict you created. It may not be very satisfying to you as the writer either.

There's nothing wrong with a silly ending. And characters don't have to get what they want. Think about how you can resolve the conflict, whether the ending is happy, sad, or something else. Try writing a few different endings to see which one you like best.

WRITING PROMPT: EXPERIMENT WITH ENDINGS

Write a short drama about this kitten and its favorite toy. You could write about how it got this toy or how it lost the toy but found it again. Then try writing three different endings. Decide which ending you like best.

As you write your ending scenes, consider the hero and villain characters in your drama. Who winds up winning and losing the conflict? How do the characters feel about what happened? Maybe you need two final scenes. The first could come from one character's perspective. The very last scene of the drama could show a different character's point of view. Do either of their perspectives alter the ending of the drama?

The final line will stick with the audience. Consider something that inspires tears, thoughts, or a burst of laughter. Think about how you want people to feel as they leave the performance. When you have finished all the steps in the writing process, your drama is ready for showtime!

WRITING PROMPT: LAST LINE

Imagine that two characters have sent each other gifts. One is the hero of the story, and the other is the villain. How would they each feel about their gifts? Write a short drama about these two characters, including dialogue so each can say thank you in their own way. End the story with a memorable final line.

GLOSSARY

cast: to assign parts to actors

climax: the most important and exciting part of a story

conflict: forces that oppose each other to create drama

dialogue: conversation in a story

draft: an early version of a piece of writing

edit: to correct or improve a piece of writing

evaluate: to carefully review, study, or judge something, such as a story

feedback: reaction to a piece of writing

perspective: a character's point of view in relation to the story

publish: to make available to the public, such as in a newspaper or magazine

revise: to change or rewrite a piece to improve it

scene: a situation in a play, movie, or show

script: written text of a play, movie, or show

stage direction: instructions written in the text of a play, such as how an actor should move or speak a line

LEARN MORE

Britannica Kids: Drama
https://kids.britannica.com/kids/article/drama/353066

Holleran, Leslie. *Writing Fiction*. Lerner Publications, 2026.

Kiddle: Drama Facts for Kids
https://kids.kiddle.co/Drama

Neely, Jenna. *Writing Skills*. World Book, 2024.

PBS Kids: Write and Perform a Play
https://www.pbs.org/parents/crafts-and-experiments/write-and-perform-a-play

Prentice, Andrew, and Matthew Oldham. *Write Your Own Scripts*. Usborne, 2023.

Rebman, Nick. *Writing Fiction*. Focus Readers, 2024.

Time for Kids: The Hero's Journey
https://www.timeforkids.com/g56/the-heros-journey-g5/?rl=en-820

INDEX

act, 6

climax, 6, 24, 26
conflict, 16, 18, 24, 26, 28

dialogue, 4, 12–14, 16, 20, 22, 28
draft, 5, 20, 22

ending, 26–28

hero, 28

metaphor, 12–13
mood, 14, 17

perform, 4–5, 28
perspective, 16–17, 22, 28
prop, 10
publishing, 5

resolve, 18, 24, 26
revise, 5, 20, 22, 25
revision, 5

script, 4
set, 10
simile, 12–13
stage direction, 12

villain, 28

PHOTO ACKNOWLEDGMENTS

Image credits: Russ Schleipman/Getty Images, p. 4; Chris Rogers/Getty Images, p. 6; FG Trade/Getty Images, p. 7; Jacob Wackerhausen/Getty Images, p. 9; Andersen Ross Photography Inc/Getty Images, p. 11; Yellow Dog Productions/Getty Images, p. 13; John M Lund Photography Inc/Getty Images, p. 15; skynesher/Getty Images, p. 16; Orbon Alija/Getty Images, p. 17 (top); NoSystem images/Getty Images, p. 17 (bottom); s-cphoto/Getty Images, p. 19; Alan Schein/Getty Images, p. 21; Ascent Xmedia/Getty Images, p. 23; Shannon Fagan/Getty Images, p. 24; SrdjanPav/Getty Images, p. 25; Kilito Chan/Getty Images, p. 27; Elva Etienne/Getty Images, p. 29. Design elements: Olex Runda/Shutterstock; Claudio Divizia/Shutterstock.

Cover: SeventyFour/Shutterstock.